T0194135

Simple Prayers

&

Bible Stories

Anne Hayward

WESTBOW
PRESS®
A DIVISION OF THOMAS NELSON
& ZONDERVAN

Interior Image Credit: https://www.pexels.com/

WestBow Press books may be ordered through booksellers or by contacting:

WestBow Press
A Division of Thomas Nelson & Zondervan
1663 Liberty Drive
Bloomington, IN 47403
www.westbowpress.com
1 (866) 928-1240

ISBN: 978-1-9736-2763-0 (sc)
ISBN: 978-1-9736-2764-7 (e)

Print information available on the last page.

WestBow Press rev. date: 05/09/2018

Acknowledgements.

Firstly, I would like to thank my wonderful husband, Clive, for all his support and proof-reading and his patience while I was writing this book. Then I must also thank Johnny and his stalwart team of instructors at the Computer Club in Pathways, at the Stockwell Head Baptist Church for all their expertise and patience, without which I would have been unable to complete the manuscript on computer.

Most of all, I thank God for giving me the ideas and impetus to attempt this, and His encouragement and love surrounding me when I felt I could not achieve this project.

Finally, a word of thanks for the staff at Westbow Press for their guidance and patience when I kept getting the format wrong!

Philippians 4, verses 6 and 7: "Do not be anxious about anything, but in everything, by prayer and petition, with thanksgiving, present your requests to God. And the peace of God, which transcends all understanding, will guard your hearts and your minds in Christ Jesus [N.I.V version]

Contents

The Lost Son.

Jesus told a story about a man whose son had moved away from home. Every day that father watched for his son to come back, and one day, he did! How happy that father was to see his son again, safe and well.

Luke 15, verses 11-24

There's a sense of loss when a child leaves home,
There's an empty space and an empty chair.
Their toothbrush has gone, and their brush and comb:
No secrets to tell, no troubles to share.
As you long for a hug, a smile and a word,
You can't wait for the day when their footsteps are heard.

Luke 15, verse 20: "…..he ran to his son, threw his arms around him and kissed him"

Prayer:

I sometimes forget where my children live and yet I still love them and am so happy to see them. Please help me to remember the good times we had together. Amen.

The Wise Man

One day, a wise man decided to build a house for himself. He surveyed for the best place, dug the foundations on rock, and eventually it was finished. When a violent storm came, he was safe and secure. Jesus said we must build our lives on the solid foundation of God's word and we, too, will be safe whatever comes our way.

Matthew 7, verse 24: "Therefore everyone who hears these words of mine and puts them into practice is like a wise man who built his house on a rock."

Prayer:

Dear Lord Jesus, Please teach us each day how to keep on building our lives according to your word. Thank-you that you have sent your Holy Spirit to help and guide us to know and understand the truths written in the Bible. Amen.

King David's Shield

King David was afraid of being killed by his son Absalom, and he ran away into the desert. In his despair, he prayed to God for protection, and felt God's presence all around him, shielding him from danger, and he began to praise God for His loving care.

2 Samuel 15 and 16

> God, shield me and protect me from all my doubts and fears.
> Please help me to remember Your arms are firm around me
> And You will never let me go through all my earthly years

Psalm 3, verse 3: "But you are a shield around me, o Lord,"

Prayer:

Heavenly Father, sometimes I get irrational fears and just want to curl up and hide. Put your loving arms around me and remind me that you will always be my helper and my Friend in times of trouble. Amen.

Fear of the Future

In the Old Testament book of Isaiah, God says, "Do not be afraid, for I have redeemed you. I have called you by your name; you are mine". This is such a comfort to me, to know that God will never forget me because He has saved me and He knows my name because I matter to Him. (*Isaiah 43, verse 1*)

"I will not forget you. See, I have engraved you on the palms of my hands" Isaiah 49, verses 15 + 16

Prayer:

Father God, I often get confused over names, dates and places, and it bothers me. Thank-you that when I read that passage I can be reassured that I am remembered by you and known as yours. Amen.

Two Odd Shoes

Jesus told us we are not to worry about anything: it is more important to trust in God for our daily needs, and that reminded me of the day I went out wearing 2 odd shoes! No-one seemed to notice, and it was only when I came home and put my slippers on that I realized what I'd done.

Matthew 6, verse 25: "Do not worry about your life, what you will eat or drink, or about your body, what you will wear"

Prayer:

Dear Lord Jesus, when I do something that's not my usual behaviour, please help me to see the funny side of it instead of worrying what other people might think. It is You I want to please. Thank-you for loving me just the way I am. Amen.

Story of the Dirty Sieve.

There was an old lady who kept reading her Bible daily but couldn't remember what she'd read. She told her minister she wasn't going to read it again, and he took her into the garden, showed her a dirty sieve and asked her to put it under the water tap. As it became clean, he said, "That's what your Bible is doing to your soul, whether you remember it or not". She smiled and kept on reading her Bible!

John 15, verse 3: Jesus said, "You are already clean because of the word I have spoken to you"

Prayer:

It's so easy to forget what I've done or read, but, Lord, draw me close to yourself and wash me as I read or listen to the passages from the Bible. Please make me more like Jesus as I think about His words. Amen.

Confusion of Night and Day.

In the winter, it is so easy to become confused about day or night. If I fall asleep in my chair and wake up suddenly, I see the time is 7 o'clock, and begin to prepare my breakfast, not realizing its evening! This makes my family laugh, but it's really not very funny to me: I feel so sad, but God tells me He knows all about me and He will wipe away my tears, and that is so good to know.

Jeremiah 31, verse 13: "I will turn their mourning into gladness; I will give them comfort and joy instead of sorrow."

Prayer:

Father God, thank-you for sending Jesus to fulfil all Your precious promises to me. Teach me to accept what I cannot change and be joyful in Your constant care for me. Amen.

A Changing World and Faith.

There is so much change in the world, and so little to depend on. God's laws are not upheld, and there is crime everywhere. Who can we trust anymore? Thank God, He remains the same. His plans will come to fruition, His purposes will be fulfilled, and His promise to send Jesus to rule as Judge and King forever is sound. All we need is a little faith, and assurance of this hope, and all because of the matchless love of God to those He has redeemed.

Faith

Hope

Love

Psalm 56, verse 3: "When I am afraid, I will trust in You"

Prayer:

Father, my faith is in You, my hope is in Jesus and the love You give me by Your Spirit sustains and fills me with joy and peace. My heart keeps on singing praises to You. Amen.

A Happy Heart.

In the book of Proverbs there is a lot of good advice, and when I read some of the verses they make me smile and cheer me up. It is good to smile: it is very contagious! When I see someone smile, I can't help but smile also. By being cheerful we can affect other people's lives and help them along the way.

Proverbs 15, verse 13: "A happy heart makes the face cheerful, but heartache crushes the spirit"

Prayer:

Thank-you, Lord Jesus for the happiness that knowing you brings. Please use me to bring joy into someone's life today, and keep me praising you as I spend my time all through this day. Amen.

Let the Children come to Me.

Jesus saw His disciples turning away the mothers who wanted him to bless their children, and he rebuked them. He called the little ones and said that the kingdom of heaven belonged to such as these. How happy that day were the mothers and their children: they would always remember that special blessing!

Luke 18, verse 16: "Let the little children come to me"

Prayer:

Lord Jesus, please welcome me as You welcomed the children long ago. Make my heart pure and simple like that of a little child so I, too, may inherit Your kingdom through Your grace and mercy. Amen.

Getting Lost – Panicking.

I remember when I got lost - it was an awful feeling and I started to panic but then I sent an urgent prayer up to God, and my heart stopped racing. Someone saw my distress and came to help me find my way back. Isn't that just like Jesus did when He came to this earth to show us the way back to God?

Ezekiel 34, verse 11: (God) says, "I myself will search for my sheep and look after them"

Prayer:

Dear Father God, thank-you for all your loving care. I know I am safe for ever because You have said you will look after me. Amen.

Saying the Wrong Thing!

When Philip told Nathaniel he had found the long-awaited Messiah, and that Jesus had come from Nazareth, Nathaniel said, "Can anything good come from there?", but when he met Jesus for himself, he knew he'd said the wrong thing! He said, "You are the Son of God" Saying the wrong thing is something I often do: I call a plant by the wrong name or mix things up, so I know how poor old Nathaniel felt! It can be very embarrassing!

Proverbs 25, verse 11: "A word aptly spoken is like apples of gold in settings of silver"

Prayer:

Lord, you know everything about me: you know my heart. When I say the wrong thing, please help those who have heard it not to judge me unkindly, but show me love and understanding. Amen.

A Land of Good Things.

There's a hymn which quotes, "The Lord has given a land of good things, I will press on, and make them mine" and today I feel happy at the thought of all the wonderful promises God has made. All I have to do is claim them for my own by faith. Life IS good when we live by faith, putting our trust in the knowledge of God's love and provision for each one who believes in Jesus.

Deuteronomy 8, verse 7: "For the Lord your God is bringing you into a good land"

Prayer:

Thank-you, Father God, for giving me happiness in this life and the promise of joy for ever in the good land after this life is over and You bring me to heaven's shore. Thank-you for the gift of faith that assures me of Your love. Amen.

The Greatest of these is Love.

Someone I know once said, "if things don't change, they'll stay as they are", and on the occasions when I lose things, or people I know and love go away, it's such a traumatic time, and I really long for things to be as they were before. I still have my faith and hope, and there is one other important thing in my life that will never change and that is God's amazing love!

Corinthians 13, verse 13: "And now these three remain: faith, hope and love. But the greatest of these is love"

Prayer:

Thank-you so much, dear God, for the abundance of Your love. I don't understand why You should love ME so much, but I am forever grateful and want to keep on saying "thank-you" all my life. Amen.

Amazing Grace.

When John Newton was in a time of crisis in his life, he called on God to save him. Years later, reflecting on God's goodness and grace, he wrote the hymn Amazing Grace, which describes the trials of his life and his trust in God which helped him through and gave him hope of many good things reserved for him in heaven.

I searched for peace and joy and love: my seeking was
    in vain
Until I found the answer to my own heart's sin and
    shame;
I found my Saviour, He found me, and gave me faith
    to see
His mighty love had brought me life,
His death had set me free.

---

1 Peter 1, verse 4: we inherit, through Jesus, "an inheritance that can never perish, spoil or fade kept in heaven for you"

Prayer:

Father God, thank-you for the witness and writings of people like John Newton who came to Jesus and found all they had been searching for. Thank-you that I came to Jesus, also, and found in Him my Saviour and Friend. Amen.

Martha and Mary.

Martha and Mary were sisters, but were so different: one was always busy, the other was keen to sit and learn, and Jesus loved them both. We have seasons in our own lives when we are very busy and become worn-out with our many duties, then later on as we grow older we have more time to meditate and to enjoy the birds and flowers.

Matthew 11, verse 28: Jesus said, "Come to me, all you who are weary and burdened, and I will give you rest"

Prayer:

Thank-you, Jesus for your constant love : when I am busy or resting, you are always beside me. Help me to work for you, like Martha, and spend time at your feet like Mary, to replenish my soul. Amen.

The Old Rugged Cross.

I do love to sing the old hymns! Isn't it strange -yet wonderful- that no matter what I forget, I can still sing the hymns of my childhood from memory. One abiding "oldie" is George Bennard's classic: The Old Rugged Cross, with its chorus, "so I'll cherish the old rugged cross, till my trophies at last I lay down. I will cling to the old rugged cross, and exchange it someday for a crown".

Paul wrote, in Colossians1, verses 20-22, that, through the blood of Jesus on the cross, God made peace and reconciled us to himself, "to present you holy in his sight"

Prayer:

Dear God, please help me to cherish the cross because Jesus suffered so much there to bring me into your presence, cleansed and precious in your sight because of his sacrificial love. Amen.

Jesus: Our Unchanging Friend.

Our weather is so changeable: one day warm and sunny, the next it's pouring with rain. We never know what to wear if we haven't heard the local weather forecast, but isn't it grand to think that at all times of day or night, winter or summer, Jesus remains just the same: our loving, caring Friend who never disappoints us.

> It's good to know that Jesus is my Friend; to be assured His love will never end,
> To know the wonders of my sins forgiven and of the joys awaiting me in Heaven.

Jesus said: "Heaven and earth will pass away, but my words will never pass away" Mark 13, verse 31

Prayer:

Thank-you, Lord Jesus, for being such a wonderful Friend to me. Your words and promises do not change with the wind, and I can truly rely on you all the time. Amen.

Guide me, O Thou Great Jehovah.

William Williams, from Pantycelyn, a farmhouse near Llandovery in Wales, wrote "Guide me, O Thou Great Jehovah", later set to the tune "Cwm Rhondda". It depicts the life of a pilgrim travelling from earth to heaven in a celebration of faith in God who hears and answers our prayer and that of the Israelites on their journey from Egypt to Canaan.

Exodus 13, verse 21: "By day, the Lord went ahead of them in a pillar of fire to guide them"

Prayer:

Lord God, you walk in front to guide me and protect me from all attacks and surround me with your loving-kindness. There is no-one greater in love, mercy and power. I am lost without you, and most truly blessed with You, and I thank you for your constant guidance in my life. Amen.

The Potter's House.

When Jeremiah went to the Potter's house, he saw a ruined piece of clay on the wheel. Instead of throwing it away, the potter started again and remade it into another pot. Isn't that just how God works in the lives of His people, moulding them to fit the task He wants them to do?

Job 10, verses 8 and 9: "Your hands shaped me and made me...you moulded me like clay"

Prayer:

Father God, I am reminded of that song, "You are the Potter and I am the clay. Help me to be willing to let you have your way; Jesus, you are changing me as I let you reign supreme within my heart".

That's my prayer today, Lord. Amen.

The Paralysed Man.

There were 5 young men who were good friends. One became paralysed, and the others tried to look after him. One day, they heard that Jesus of Nazareth could heal people, and they carried his stretcher to the house where Jesus was teaching. They couldn't get in because of the crowd, so they made a hole in the roof and lowered their friend to Jesus – and he healed him! How thrilling was that!

A man in despair, in a desperate plight,
Inactive and sad from morning to night
Just dreaming of past days when he'd run and walk,
Yet blessed to have 4 friends to visit and talk.
They took him to Jesus, and then, straightaway
His sins were forgiven, and he walked away.

Matthew 9, verse 6: (Jesus) said, "Get up, take your mat and go home"

Prayer:

Thank-you, Jesus, for being so full of love and compassion, and always willing to help all who come to you in faith: teach us to expect miracles, and to praise you when you meet our needs. Amen.

Tears in His Bottle.

Why would anyone want to collect tears? In the Bible we read, "He has put all my tears in His bottle. *(Psalm 56, verse 8)* I thought of some of the types of tears: sadness, happiness, compassion, loneliness, grief, despair, and the tears of joy when a new baby is born. We all cry, and God records all the times we weep, and He's there with us as we shed those tears, comforting, and rejoicing, helping and providing. What a personal God is ours! Let's praise Him for being so close to us!

Psalm 126, verse 5: "Those who sow tears shall reap joy"

Prayer:

Father God, thank-you for loving me so much. Amen.

Green Tomatoes.

There are such a lot of green tomatoes left in the greenhouse. What use are they? You can't eat them in a salad, so should they be thrown away? Oh, no! They make wonderful green tomato chutney, and the longer it matures, the better the flavour. Praise God, He doesn't throw us away when we feel of no use any more: He uses us in a different way to work for Him and bring Him glory. I'm always of use to my Lord: even in sickness or disability I can praise Him for His goodness in my life.

1 Thessalonians 5, verse 24: "The one who calls you is faithful, and he will do it"

Prayer:

Dear God, please encourage me today by making me useful to you by my cheerfulness and patience in spite of how my body is aching. Keep me faithful to share how much you mean to me. Amen.

Wonders of Creation.

How lovely to see a sunset after a beautiful day! Such an abundance of colours and the different shades in the clouds make me wish I could paint them to remind me of that scene for ever. How many people stop to consider this is the work of God's hands, and his blessing of sight is given to enjoy all He created. The sweet songs of birds are a blessing to those whose vision is impaired, yet few appreciate the senses we are born with. A pig's eyes are so placed that he cannot see the sky. What a shame that is. Today, let us thank God for all the work of His hands.

Psalm 40, verse 5: "Many, O Lord my God, are the wonders you have done"

Prayer:

Thank-you for the world so sweet, thank-you for the food we eat. Thank-you for the birds that sing. Thank-you, God, for everything. Amen. Author: E. Rutter Leatham

A New Heart.

In December, 1967 in a South African hospital, Christiaan Barnard performed the first heart transplant. This reminds me of the promise of God to transform hearts of stone into hearts of love for Him: what a transplant that will be! We will truly know how to love with all our hearts, and never be unhappy again. That's amazing, isn't it?

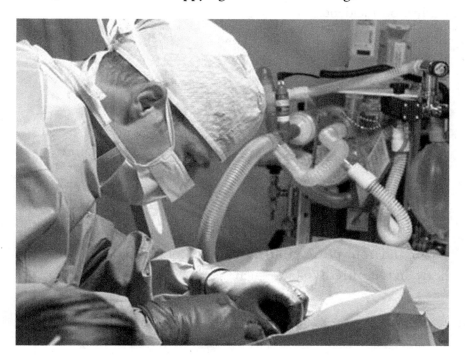

Ezekiel 11, verse 19: "I will remove from them their heart of stone and give them a heart of flesh"

Prayer:

Please, Lord, soften my heart and help me to show love to others just like in the hymn *"A heart like Thine, a heart divine, a heart as white as snow; on me, dear Lord, a heart like this bestow". Amen. *Written by George Jackson

I am the Lord.

In the book of Ezekiel, God wanted to impress on the people of Israel that all the disasters that would come upon their nation were for the purpose of God's punishment for their idolatry. He stressed 70 times throughout the book, "Then they will know I am the Lord" so they would be aware that what could be thought of as coincidences were really God-incidents.

"I am the LORD"

Ezekiel 6, verse 14: "Then they will know I am the Lord"

Prayer:

Dear Lord, I want to know You NOW, to know Your presence, Your power and Your peace in my life. Please come, Lord Jesus, into my heart and life afresh today. Amen.

Mountains.

Mountains: they can be obstacles or viewing points, depending on your perception of them. We all have mountains to climb and obstacles to get over during our life-time. Moses had Mount Sinai and Mount Gerizim, (for blessing) and Mount Ebal (for cursing) *Deuteronomy 27, verses 12 and 13.*

Psalm 121, verses 1 and 2: "I lift up my eyes to the hills – where does my help come from? My help comes from the Lord, the Maker of heaven and earth."

Prayer:

Dear God, sometimes I feel there is a mountain in front of me that's too hard to climb, and too wide to go around. Please help me put things in perspective and rely on You to help me to cope. Amen.

Gardens.

What do you think of when a garden is mentioned? Is it a lovely, peaceful haven with lots of flowers and benches to sit on, or is it an untended plot that's full of weeds and rubbish? The Garden of Eden was a beautiful place. It must have been a joy for Adam and Eve to cultivate until sin entered and they were sent away to toil endlessly over brambles and weeds. Our lives are like gardens: we can choose to fill them with good things or let sinful thoughts and acts thrive in them. God can make us good gardeners if we invite Him to share our lives each day.

John 15, verse 1: "I am the true Vine and my Father is the gardener"

Prayer:

Please come into my life and make it beautiful for you. Amen.

The Light of the World.

In the Bible, David was feeling lost and confused, and then he turned to God in prayer, and wrote these words of faith and hope, "The Lord is my light and my salvation: whom shall I fear?"

(Psalm 27, verse 1)

John 8, verse 12: (Jesus) said, "I am the light of the world. Whoever follows me will never walk in darkness, but will have the light of life."

Prayer:

Dear God, I often feel lost and confused. Please help me to come to you, my heavenly Father, for your comfort and peace. Amen.

God's Creation.

God created a wonderful world, and it is by his power that it is sustained. He created man in his own image, and gave him the job of caring for the environment and all living creatures. We often do not see the beauty of the world around us.

Genesis 2, verse 15: "The Lord God took the man and put him in the Garden of Eden to work it and take care of it"

Prayer:

Forgive me, Lord, for neglecting to see the beauty of creation all around me. Thank-you for all that you have made, including me. Amen.

Holy Communion.

Paul reminded the Christians at Corinth to be respectful of other worshippers and to remind each other of the sacrifice of Jesus every time they took bread and wine at their communion service.

1 Corinthians 11, verse 26: "For whenever you eat this bread and drink this cup you proclaim the Lord's death until he comes"

Prayer:

Please, Lord, help me to remember how much you love me, and the great sacrifice you made on my behalf. Amen.

The Birth of Jesus.

In the Gospel of Luke, we read of shepherds who were looking after their sheep. An angel appeared to them and told them of the birth of Jesus in a stable in Bethlehem. Suddenly, they saw a host of angels and heard them singing praises to God. The shepherds went quickly to look for the Baby.

(Luke 2, verses 8-16)

A Baby in a manger, with cattle standing by,
A shining star that shone up in the velvet sky;
Shepherds heard the angels sing
An anthem to the new-born King:
This story old yet ever new,
That Christ was born for me and you,
Our Saviour-God, the Prince 0f Peace.
Oh, may His praises never cease!

Isaiah 9, verse 6: "For to us a child is born, to us a son is given, and the government will be on his shoulders. And he will be called Wonderful Counselor, Mighty God, Everlasting Father, Prince of Peace."

Prayer:

Thank-you, Lord Jesus, for coming to live and die to save me from my sins. Please help me to remember how very much you love me. Amen.

Don't Worry!

Jesus told us not to worry about food, drinks, or what clothes to wear because God, our heavenly Father, knows what we need and will supply it.

(Matthew 6, verse 5)

Psalm 23, verse 5: "You prepare a table before me"

Prayer:

Heavenly Father, sometimes I have forgotten whether I have eaten my dinner, and have chosen the wrong clothes to wear. Thank-you for sending people to help me. Thank-you that you always know just what I need. Amen.

The Lost Coin.

There was a woman who lost a coin, and she searched everywhere until she found it. She was so happy, called all her friends to tell them about it.
(Luke 15, verses 8+9)

Luke 15, verse 9: "Rejoice with me; I have found my lost coin"

Prayer:

Dear Lord, I often lose things, and it is very upsetting, so I can understand this woman's joy when she found what she'd lost. Thank-you that I am never lost to you and your loving care. Amen.

A Song to Sing.

We are told to sing to the Lord and give thanks to him for sending Jesus, who showed us what God's love was like. He brings us joy and peace and hope of heaven.

Colossians 3, verse 16: "Let the word of Christ dwell in you richly...as you sing psalms, hymns and spiritual songs with gratitude in your hearts to God."

Prayer:

Please, Lord, help me today to believe all your promises, and give me a song in my heart. Amen.

The Last Supper.

On the night before he was betrayed, Jesus sat and had a meal with his disciples, and told them that they were to remember him as his body being the bread of life and the wine representing his blood, shed for the salvation of all people.

Communion wine is bitter-sweet:
Wounded His hands, His side, His feet:
A crown of thorns laid on His head,
His body broken, like the bread.
It tells of love and sacrifice.
Yes, surely Jesus paid the price!
Lord, as I thus remember You,
Keep me faithful, keep me true.

Mark 14, verse 24: "This is my blood of the covenant, which is poured out for many"

Prayer:

Dear Lord Jesus, please let me always remember your death and resurrection with a grateful heart. When I forget, please let someone remind me. Amen.

How to Pray.

Jesus was asked by his disciples to teach them how to pray and so he said the words we now know as "The Lord's Prayer". I often need to remember how to pray for my own needs and to praise God for all his love and the ways he helps me each day. (Matthew 6, verses 9-12)

Mark 11, verse 24: "Whatever you ask for in prayer, believe that you have received it, and it will be yours"

Prayer:

Heavenly Father, please give me the faith to believe you are answering my prayers. Amen.

Joshua and the Walls of Jericho.

In the Old Testament, Joshua needed to capture the city of Jericho and he trusted in the plan of action God had given, even though it seemed the wrong way to fight the battle. God gave him a mighty victory and everyone was amazed.

A mighty city in the way!
But Joshua found time to pray;
He put his trust in God's good plan,
The walls fell down as trumpets rang!
A victory won, a story told –
God made them strong and made them bold.

Joshua 6, verse 27: "So the Lord was with Joshua and his fame spread throughout the land"

Prayer:

Dear God, there are times in my own life when I don't know what to do or how to ask for help. Please be with me just as you were with Joshua. Amen.

The Lord is my Shepherd.

The Lord is my shepherd; I shall not be in want. He makes me to lie down in green pastures. He leads me beside quiet waters. He restores my soul. He guides me in paths of righteousness for his name's sake.

(Psalm 23, verses 1-3)

John 10, verse 14: Jesus said, "I am the good shepherd"

Prayer:

I need someone to look after me. Sometimes I feel anxious and afraid. Please, Lord Jesus, be my shepherd and guide and help me today. Amen.

Jesus in the Storm.

Jesus and his disciples were in a boat on the lake, and suddenly a violent storm blew up. Jesus was fast asleep, and they were terrified they might drown. When they woke him, Jesus calmed the storm and they all arrived safely ashore. *(Mark 4, verses 35-41)*

When the waves are high and the wind blows strong
It's very hard to sail along;
But when the words of God speak, "Peace!"
Even hurricanes will cease.
Don't be alarmed at storms within:
No boat's capsized with Jesus in!

Matthew 8, verse 26: "Then (Jesus) got up and rebuked the winds and the waves, and it was completely calm."

Prayer:

Lord Jesus, there are times in my own life when I feel as if I am in a storm, and I am so frightened. Please speak your words of peace to my heart, and let me feel your calming presence in my life. Amen.

Eternal Life.

There were some Christians who were unsure of what happened when they died. Paul wrote to reassure them that Jesus has promised them eternal life in heaven with him. We can also have this hope of being forever with the Lord because of his great love and faithfulness.

> Eternal life! No pain, no tears, no death, a home where
>   all is peace.
> Our Saviour-God has promised us a place where wars
>   will cease.
> How wonderful the thought of this, where there's no
>   sin and shame;
> We'll meet with loved ones who, like us, have loved the
>   Saviour's name.
> Eternity will seem too short to glorify and praise
> Our Triune God through all the endless days.
> There's no night there, nor waves nor storm,
> And none can do His children harm.
> Oh, Praise the Lord for all He's done:
> For journey's end and battles won.

1 Thessalonians 5, verse 10: "[Jesus Christ], who died for us that...we should live together with him"

Prayer:

Dear Lord, please help me to remember that you have promised me a home with you in heaven one day. Thank-you for your loving care every day of my life. Amen.

God's Son Shines.

There's a little ditty that goes, "we'll weather the weather whatever the weather, whether we like it or not!" Some days the weather just doesn't suit us: too hot, too cold, too wet, too windy; but we just have to put up with it, and moaning certainly isn't going to help! In the Bible we read of Jesus being the Light of the world, and he testifies of himself, "I am the bright Morning Star" *(Revelation 22, verse 16)*. If we look to him instead of inclement weather, our day will become brighter. Jesus, God's Son, shines in our hearts and our lives as we seek his face.

1 John 1, verse 5: "In him there is no darkness at all"

Prayer:

Thank-you, Jesus, for being a light in my life, chasing away the darkness of doubt and despair and bringing me hope and peace. Help me to shine for you today in all I say and do. Amen.

Joy of the Harvest.

There's something quite special about growing plants from seeds or bulbs: a feeling of achievement when flowers bloom and vegetables and fruit become ripe. Even people who have no garden-space can grow plants on a window-sill! I grew some carrots in an old plastic mop-bucket, and they were small but delicious. God has planted us just where we are to flourish and become fruitful for his pleasure.

Ecclesiastes 3, verse 11 tells us that God "has also set eternity in the hearts of men"

Prayer:

Father God, it is wonderful to know that you have given me everything I need to grow fruitful in your service; please continue to feed me daily on your word and help me to grow in grace that I may witness to your love and power in my life. Amen.

A Simple Gift.

Have you ever said, "I have nothing to give"? That's just not true! God has made every one of us unique and has given us special gifts. If you can cheer someone up or help someone, or say a prayer when you see a need, this comes from a heart of love, and is a God-given gift. It takes a special person like you to see a need and minister to it. You have been used by God for his glory in the world. How humbling and thrilling is that!

1 Corinthians 9, verse 12: "This service that you perform is not only supplying the needs of God's people but is also overflowing in many expressions of thanks to God"

Prayer:

Lord God, I feel so humbled at the thought of never being too old or frail to be of use to you. It's amazing that you still have work I can do for you. Please strengthen me for your service, I pray. Amen.

Outlook.

What is your outlook on life? Some people look in a mirror and moan, majoring on their ailments and woes, and some look out of the window and view with interest what's going on around them in spite of their ailments and difficulties. Do you look back at yourself or out at others? Caring and concern should be paramount for a Christian, and to live each moment showing the love of Jesus to all we meet. It's not easy, but it is possible with God at work in us.

Matthew 5, verse 16: "Let your light shine among men"

Prayer:

Dear Lord, I remember singing "let your little light shine" when I was a child. Now I am old, please let my light still be shining and lighting the way for others to come to you to receive light and joy in their lives, too. Amen.

Everything is Beautiful.

The words of the song, "Everything is beautiful in its own way" is one of my favourite songs. I am reminded of the different kinds of beauty: in flowers, in meadows and woods, the beauty of a rainbow, the way dew-drops glitter in the sunlight, the beauty in a baby's smile and the laughter of little children, but most of all the beauty of a life made clean by Jesus.

Ecclesiastes 3, verse 11: "He has made everything beautiful"

Prayer:

Dear God, please open my eyes to see the beauty all around me, and help me to see more clearly the beauty of Christ. "Let the beauty of Jesus be seen in me" Make this the longing of my heart today. Amen.

A Prayer or a Pray-er?

It is easy to pray from a prayer-book, but it is not always what you want to say. Simply tell God what is on your heart. The Bible tells us that he is "nearer than hands or feet", and that's pretty close! His ear is always open to hear you and if "his eye is on the sparrow", then certainly his eye is on you because you are precious to him. Talk to him now, and be confident that he will hear and answer your prayer.

Philippians 4, verses 6+7: "Do not be anxious about anything, but in everything, by prayer and petition, with thanksgiving, present your requests to God.

Prayer:

Thank-you, Jesus, for being my Friend who shares all my troubles and knows all my weakness, who helps me and cheers me and on whom I can totally rely. You are always listening to the cry of my heart. I love you, Lord. Thank-you for loving me. Amen.

Justified by Faith.

An elderly minister once told me that the word "justified" wasn't difficult to understand when it was divided into "just *as* if I'd *never sinned*". That has stuck with me for over 60 years: I forget many facts and figures, but I still remember this! Jesus made my life just as if I'd never sinned. I don't deserve his love and sacrifice, but I'm forever grateful that he died for me. I want to live for him until my final breath. Trust him today and let him justify you and give you peace.

> Oh, Praise the Lord! He rescued me: He paid the price on Calvary.
> I'm justified by faith alone, my hope and trust in Him are found;
> No works or penance, prayers or tears could ever set me free.
> The finished work by Jesus paid have set my feet on higher ground.

Romans 5, verse 1: "we have been justified by faith"

Prayer:

Thank-you, Jesus, for paying the ransom for me. I know I'm a sinner, but you have saved me and brought me into a right relationship with God. Please make me ever mindful of your grace and mercy. Amen.

Printed in the United States
By Bookmasters